Hieronymus Square

Jacob Kobina Ayiah Mensah

Contents

Hieronymus Square

1.

We wait here to see if we too can slip away into the next house,
this house which is larger than the country it is built in. Where
everybody can take clemency for weakness and difference of opinion
for crime. This is the house we still wait next exhibition
in their disappointment. Tomato plant is growing on the radiator
and they dislike this understanding. I remember the marks of their eyes
and how they have been painted in reds with Indian ink, and white clay,
and on the cheeks and you aspire to be one, you whose
virtues are odious passions, that are twisted round,
we climb the floating staircase to the last floor.
We see what we see with their sockets ahead of us,
I manage with your hands, woman, those hands you have stolen
from this square, this vigil, and your referee too is waiting
doggedly for what may follow. I see what he has said
having no effect on us when his right hands produce
a foolscap street to show a new direction, I cherish
this artistic composition and his gentleman in the way
he signs his name in a form of folding a large letter.
Now that we demand our price, we hang our pictures
in the Bureau separately or collectively with your head
in human, I break the silence you have built around
my failed body, I see nothing more than ridiculous
colours painted on the walls, you push me back into
a corner, from which, as often as I stand up into the plank,
I persist in emerging again from your wound, you say
I need patience and follow the common the thin line
that divides the mind and the heart for a measure.
This is the daily trial we go through to find out about

the teaspoons if they sum up to execute any conceptions
of your paintings which are too feeble, they describe them,
this unfortunate rendering of everything I have kept
for his hour have a look inside to see how it works
and in what conditions it is, I wedge the paper firmly,
forgetting that the pictures on the floor are swallowing me.
I feel sure that the early symptoms are unmistakable
when your appearance is no longer quite under your control.
I loss your face, that dims, your skin that used to coarsen
also dimes, I cope with all these things and how you
have neglected yourself, I am drifting apart, and tireless
you are and transferring this to me and them, I have
noticed how this dogma and immaculate and irrelevant
your stand seems as the whole thing dropping from the ceiling.
Can I appoint a stoker and supply him kerosene for the burning?
I light up the lawns with a torch though it is still noon,
I wake up those who are still sleeping the park buried
in the snowdrift, we begin a new winter under your peaceful
outlook of my childhood, I still remember with your conscience.
I blame everything for all the misfortunes that follow the glittering
phrases in your teeth, I imagine that this is out of date, what
the viewers say about these pictures, I legalize their mouths.
I close the bottle for we are not yet openly hostile to each other.

2.

Three drops of water spread across the whole floor
and you wonder why this is possible at this hour
when roaring voices are deafening and there is
a sudden lull, and the clucking behind the wall
becomes isolated words among moving shadows,
we calmly stretch our strength to empty the wet,
the room remains in a lit by the guttering candle.
Having this copy here, plainly before the big eyes,
I replace my handkerchief in your pocket for intent
expression all the while to form something different
from your supposition in folly when the candle eyes
sparkle up in your hands you smite over the fire,
busily stirring, I rub my hands in relief from recent
happenings, feelings on the shoulders, I hint on
no objection for similar reasons I make how we
exclaim, laying down on the edge of a sharp knife,
I cannot help wondering in my imagination to glue
that joints for carving all that at sixties, I think
they are in consequence or to display indifference
after making numerous mistakes accustomed to that
occupation for strengthening a distinguished suite,
you wonder why the doctor has taken these lenses
for all these hours to begin the next morning at
seven o'clock when the rest of his staff consider

his discontented looks at the table with actions
and passions mixed to inquire your taste that has
become so obvious before the first performance.
Now that we hide our identities below this darkness,
let this body I wear with your support remain its frame
from stains and pains and not ought to be amused
or entertained those who are engaging you to conclude
your outlook for cultural acquisition, which is necessary
to be professed as a small moment in their various
pursuits, I alter my appetite to apprehend the malady
on this floor with satisfying proceedings, beginning
with a prodigious sacrifice, impatience, scented soap
and cold water to wash hands free, I take acute finishing
line to my reverses, I consult no debates, no reference
to any partnership, I entreat everything, stupid or good,
to myself for your satisfaction to be observed by his spare
company under the tarpaulin like a white vulture, gorging
around his shadow to be disc loused for a certain prospect,
I know how you love with your own lips, regarding yourself
the innocent of best course for peace and other conclusion.

3.

The large days are unheard in his pockets.
He keeps them like vodka and indulges
in grandiloquent sentences to dilute
a small portion of his life according to his
inspiration to hold a large number of varying
strength to annoy everybody who enters
this bar, especially, during the odd hours,
when rank-and-file workers take the corners.
It is discovered that within the next few days
his expense is secured to play the fool and old
order for genuine characters, who are emerging
from the next moment and a wretched existence.
This street fighting is at its height. Guns are
common, and the city is suspended to ease
your suffering when your child is dead at
their raspberry larynx and outside the gates,
I am released from their three days by enter-
training them with pointless talk to see them go.
Cops operations continue, streets are still closed,
two strangers are killed by stray bullets, you are
out, he has gotten through by vomiting this time,
he buries everything, including the world within.
You stay outside the bar because it is not opened,
you talk for hours with the cops, things do not

progressed, you develop a sore throat and a fever.
Just last week, your boys were arrested for possessing
guns unlawfully. Tonight, you are out yourself,
aiding the cops with your ribs and guts. Now that
your collogue is far off his space, what is the next
move from here to the next day to prove yourself?
You hear gun shots, another group has joined the contest,
the cops look for a cover and everything vanishes
beyond the horizon and suddenly reappears in a broad
at a turn, however, you have gotten to use it, this
intersection, they are coming in to this on business.
Thinking alone this time to have everything from
exhaustion that comes with crossing the yard in
a change of name, I bear the weight of your narrator
at the police station and keep the dig the eyes, staring
in every corner and I erase the distance with your thinking.
Because I am ambiguous, I strive with the Gospel to
contrast every commonplace for birth and life that follows.

4.

She has become everything, she my grandmother.
She is visible, audible, a complete picture for those
who have returned from the prisons, those who seek
employment in her tomato farms, she encourages them
to redraw themselves with airbrush, charcoal, sanguine,
and chalk, she tells them to prepare for any domestic trial,
she is also about the little sums she has made from
the oldest inhabitants, who engage her in conversation.
I cannot have the present occasion for a little more room
I have wished for a prettier wife, who sits at the opposite
the mahogany table, I have heard about all the news.
I seem to pursue my grandmother's figure through this drama,
I take the chair she has handed me, I hear no tap at the door.
Her face impresses me, having gradually removed from my eyes,
she raises her eyes when I lay my hand on the shoulder of a shadow,
she offers on meaning but remains throughout perfectly still.
Knowing how to utter hopelessness from attention that holds
us from the distance when the main gate is opened and the street
is in front of everything you touch without thinking about it,
I recollect some fierce things, that continue to drag the length
of her wishing someone who is running from the field toward the gate.

5.

At Pocatello, where our real faces are kept for profit,
I manage my time to see what has been taken away
from these our other selves from the same on the market.

It is here their stupidity has been shaped among the natives
they have favoured and moulded with a language of insubstantiality,
the task of this translation remains all the sunshine that is gone.

6.

I have the formation to create new words that
are abstract words deliberately coined from
objects or practically unamenable to language,
something that chessmen do to describe inner
life on the chess board after a dream fails to exist.
Major facts in a language are that no concrete
is visible. It is the large guesswork to remove
a word from its exertion than that of its heightening.
I persuade the much less provision we doubt its
sincerity because we firmly rely on the liberality,
I hold my intentions according to your intimacy.
Fortunately, a word's abilities is left to its wishes,
or disposition to attain its height or concerns.
You have called enough from these peculiar
circumstances by striking their taste and purity.
This is the shortest day to store up light from the sun,
you spread your love built on canonization, I add
my gout, I wonder by such a pilgrimage under a lens.
From here you gather dresses from words I form,
you describe their security fences and mount a barrier
by balancing man and woman from a ladder.
I lean against a pomegranate tree in the weedy world.

7.

I have lent my son to God.
A remark that seems to wake
my neighbours and bring them to life.

8.

Half way down this room,
I look at the faces on the wall
that once supported the incalculable moments

that swilling into years of incredibly echoes
for selfless beginnings,
so spare, so vicious in the hospital.

He sleeps on the couch
and that adjustment is well worth it,
he forges friendships on construction projects.

Volunteer when disasters strike!
A unique privilege to feel richer from that experience!
He looks at you in a fact that never really seems yours.

In the corridor outside,
you look up and see who he is,
a figure with a curiously lethal.

Moving away from your body
that is now dying among tribal conflicts,
children play with bottle tops on the verandah.

9.

He has left his homework behind
and you and I cannot complete his life.
Vanilla taste is the only thing in my possession
I hasten away with you. Glad that you have to quit
my gloomy monitories and look at my face for the first time.

I add something without further remonstrance.

10.

My father has left the note I have written
in the wet sand and I carry this note with
me in everywhere I walk, I estimates that
its annual expenditure is partly constant
and partly varies as the distances I cover,
I find its weight equal to the weight of metal,
that memories from a fixed point per head.
Somewhere a train rounding a corner
and then to the stop, I feel alive all at once.
Suddenly, I begin to sink in the number
of people present on the platform,
and now you are here to make a difference
from recollecting the distances I have lost,
I wish to look as well as you earn a broad day.

I dress myself with your care with extreme
simplicity and not my usual habit

         to rise at the view

perhaps to carpet the floor after the flood,
or to curtain a place between the sun
and the gay blue window, you define
the careless appearance with solicitous fit.

At least recoiling from these distances
with antipathy, I consider your choice
from this small apartment to solitary,

                    I am ushered into my cold body.

A splendid raining morning
over isles among stones in long succession,
I gather sea pavements, I see the library,
still closed to strangers from a hand breath,
I have assumed a low seat near the public garden,
a flock of birds passing by.

          Somewhere under the shelter of imagination

I stop my ears against the gust.
I utter a silent prayer
for those separated by the coming grief.

The spectacle is so amicable to adopt
from the cold sunshine and your presence.

My walls are falling and I do not close the windows.
Because we are using them as exit
to where you are endowed with force,
I allow him, your houseboy, to go
through education and his position,

your mother calculates the maneuvers
from the sunbeam left behind to highlight the pale faces.
I am not forgetting all these faults
but I do not look at them,
I do not want to feel justified in judging or blaming.
This is not my work.
You draw the curtain in the sky
in the opposite to my casement.

You rise your voice against mine and say:
— What are you doing in this game beyond the light?
You're a stranger and get out of this!

      I am quiet still looking at your direction in the whirlwind

      I cut the afternoon into pieces.

I say to you: — Who cares about what we're here and at home?

It is always the same thing, the same reply
it is the autumnal body but
this is the immerse darkness
with no shadows to linger about,

      I pursue my desire
between the mind and the heart,
where a room is free for dreaming,

      I hunt in my dream

I step into a ground not far
from an ominous voice,
someone you have not known
before is waking up
in your missing body.

I go to look for Aunt Killjoy in this metallic city.
Here she lives with a pathologist, who is also
a distant relation, I come across many foundries,
I see many friendly faces coming out of the casting
to remain the lifeline of any life raft that is cut short.
We meet Lieutenant Colonel Williams, your uncle,
whose ligneous body is almost as yours for a lignite,
I prolong my stay in bed in the morning to hear him
saying all that he can to help his brother who is
jabbering, I manage the jardinére, my new assignment
with no jape I have found in the wilderness, indeed,
it is the substance and the basic guide he purposes
to restrain himself from everything he sees and not
to see it as a simple or when that seems suddenly
very simple, I take everything back until I find myself
looking at the mountains obviously with your new eyes.
I am sure something is not right in the chimney
I press for further exercise when the hysterical laugh
becomes clear in the entrance to the library hall.
I hang part of me on the frame, I read passages
of love and hate from your heart, which has become
their Bible, I solve each circle problem, since the purpose
is to uplift the people who are planting and growing trees
on their compounds and the street in front of them
to administer the sun for no moral edification before
each question we provide with religious antinode.
He tries make your children friendly to the creatures
we meet them when we continue to sketch the late
hawthorn blossom with a soft black pencil and Indian ink.
I shape everything they have from the temples to the foreheads.
The children decide the cleft down the mouth we open,

I trace it with a paper on a broad with a glimpse of sea water
between rocks, I am glad that you have come in.
The corners are garlanded, everything in the room
carries its memories, they show their dislikes and illness.

A black coat has its memory replaced by a newspaper article.

I default your will and fail to sharpen
your face for the nights and absence
to display who we are by broken faith,
the antsized yam heads in a complete
shallows are risen upward like rippling
in the wind, we wrap the sun with a piece
of wet newspaper and hurry up to the artist's
studio within a quarter of your life

He clothes his body with big mouths here
that have nothing to say, I step on a fool's shadow

I make a room for his foolishness,
stirring by grief and joy within,
you struggle for your full sway

to assert the acute right to overcome
your weakness when you cannot stand
to your anger, the island grass is in the glass
I carry to correct your seasons, I fold days
like a newspaper you have just read
to grow a new communicant who is
registering his name at 79, I carry your side,

yet to be known by them
who find it very hard to accept you.

11.

I have found a dream someone has hidden
under a grain of sand but it is soaked with
sweats and blood in a form of red mud
I am about mechanically to obey him
and help myself into the seed husk,
where your providence is blessed
and I wish to adopt your endeavours
to secure a competency. I fix my recollection.

12.

After taking the foot-candle from behind the mirror, the Night Watch
becomes a distance for only a short period and the luminous intensity
decreases by the square of this fictive distance, making us find the room
for new conventions to express new message, Rembrandt is right to

                                        create the greatest weight which can be
supported by a beam of given

thickness varies directly as the breadth and inversely as the length as

the distance travelled by the eyes

in this shooting expedition, pierced by

darkness, the formula is a subtext of free forgiveness.

I manage the gazing eyes in your clammy hands.

13.

Far from your body the mind becomes blurred.
The cells are all dead and you cannot cut through
the clouds, everything remains less observed.
We fence through the wild grass and mud
to protect our bones expose in the pilgrims
of hard core boys, who have refused to live
in classrooms, who storm here with catapults,
birds and lizards fail to share their other lives.

The Pulley and the Will

I thread a needle
with a thread of the sea,
I stitch my memory left
abandoned in the dust.
Suddenly afterglow.
The door starts from here.
I put your colour high
above my needs and about tea,
you will excuse me one moment
when we rise and leave the room for good.
A glint in your calm.
It is almost lukewarm or tepid,
someone behind this effusive smile speaks
with a slow drawl,
I presume so colourlessly.
We stare at the crumpled cup,
full of faces, flickering,
you wriggle into the contest,
he presides over the ceremony of pouring your feelings,
we find some suitable compensation for them.
The boys agree with this English climate
and I need something to stand up against
this great heat inside or that great cold outside,

I examine the pearl-like pebbles I gather from a flexibility of voices
before you translate the supper.
I feast instead on this spectacle,
full of drawings in Indian ink and darkness,
I feel my own hands falling freely
in penciled lines
in imagination prepared by your pupil.
Under the gentler breathing,
tonight temperature freezes.
I manage the order in the mirror
and speak my mind.
All that allowing another steps to commence in your life,
I learn its first two tenses,
outrivaling the new milk
in less than two months
to amuse my inward craving,
which I see in the dark,
I solve my satisfaction
with all its privations for daily luxuries
you have promoted
and hold a little longer than me,
you allow her eyes to follow the door.
She counts the number of wretched feet
left behind to be flayed and swollen
to lameness and pale gold gleam.
I wander to the impulse of the wet beach sand.
I peel my eyes to see clearly
in my desires to listen to your attendant
when her desertion has affected you,
I mark that specimen to be given out
for her accomplishment in this opera.
She lifts her blue eyes to the ceiling,
the light begins to brighten,
a portion of her heart,
she repeats me my false memory
like a guest at distinguished houses,
where a mouse squeaks,
the old door creaks, opening widely,
you hear a clock ticking.
Suddenly, you smell an orange juice, fizzing.
You look around like a detective,

you see only shadows,
waving in the dry leaves, thriving
in the shallow water, someone steps in,
splashing heavily with working boots.
I hear your presence, emerging once more
to manifest at least a little interest
in affairs not yours, I lean against the new villa suburb
above the seashore from the decaying coconut plantations.
I crunch my dry biscuits in silence
when your ladies, I mean your daughters,
jolt beside me, always out of step,
I keep the thread of my mind in order,
which is equal to resistance, R, and is 4 times
as long as any length, L, the radius, r,
remains RL/k, where k is a constant.
I build on this abstract algebra,
leaving its structure open
in your shillings at least,
a form of the wild notion to rush
your deflated figure in a curt movement
of tribal robe, the tempest in the ropes
seems at all idiotic with its curious crumpled bagginess.
I am sure you have observed this path,
the clock has struck 2.
I withdraw to the parlour.
The snow stars are pasted in the space.
Their appearance excites me so keen an interest
in a vector space,
I make an effort to compel it
to remain there in dumb and still.
I hope this is exactly how you want our lives
to take their mould and a voice quite close at hand,
such as yours will be if we perish here of want.
I am terrified at the unexpected sound
from among you, it is snowing.
A feeling of care remains on the wall,
everybody watches it morbidly
with self-consciousness this time from his apartment.
You wait at the train station, where passengers
jump out the queue and run to the next buffet,
or struggle to separate the furiously speeding of the night train

from a higher sense of bitter exception,
you maintain unwillingness to the things
yet to be remembered and erased from its presence.
Now that I wait in silent indignation,
I go on listening to the sounds approaching,
she gets through the confinement,
where it is always damp and dark,
this time becomes the weather she wears,
everybody who sees her becomes exhausted
by the whole body strains,
her eyes still follow you to the door.
In a low voice, intended to be divided
and arranged in conspicuous characters,
I burn in my whole soul,
having assembled for the next spectacle,
I solve your satisfaction
and I see them laughing rarely.
Because they demand the divine and perfect,
I am afraid I am enigmatical
when you cannot feel apprehensive.
I add that, let your features
muffle your voice
before unsanctioned line of action.
My interlocutor is beyond my penetration,
even more vivacity, or variety than
you dare to offer at intervals,
this restricting limbs are liable to abuse.
I watch her for nearly half an hour,
I change the more dissatisfied colours in this mural,
I turn a page, you miss the young single lady gipsy,
I think it must be you,
who is there no more else for it again.
Unobserved by any eye from among you,

it is raining. December is heavy on the plains.

Half-cut dash. The rate is 2.07% from the beginning.
This is gained by being read in conjunction with its
own for whom it is assumed, it is far from scorning

the commonplace question about its size, from you
where the encounters are satisfying the momentum,
its beauty is spared for his foolish little heroine to make
any energy, E, varies as the square of my taste I
measure from cappuccino to vanilla. I spill this like
water, but for nothing more than water to draft me
into the army after having much to end everything
I count from the springy birch saplings to December
mornings, you split my sides from laughing, stored.
Well, I work this long story mine and I do not know
where to begin. That white bastard waits to squeeze
blood out of the stones, eating the sea, drop by drop,
you force me to see will-o'-the-wisps in every eye,
I remain to every bone broken in the bodies in your hands.
You know where they are and you do not worry at all.
I see the light and I have done away with a lot of your kind,
one little fellow gets you out of his mind, the escort
closes around the sums in a semicircle, where prayers
and sacrifices were once offered by unknown worshippers.

The Dual

I seal names you cannot use at the registry
because they are not new names you have
not registered when your Northwest is having
a brief respite from the clouds smouldering,
we wait to have dinner in an Italian restaurant
in Seven Points. The thermometer registers 73° F.
I fix the door to the rehabilitation, you rehouse
the war refugees for a programme, I remember
nothing with your invocation, only that comfort
I point to with a pointer over and over to prepare
a long expenses when we are too conscious
of the waste of your promise with such a tenacious
modesty. I mark the ribs and guts left behind
in the rocks and the mud.

You can guess and refuse

to honour. O, I am thinking of Galois and Pushkin
who end their joylessness with trusted treasure,
O, I am thinking of this statue
approaching here with his eyes,
glistening with tears of death.

I yawn, twilight.

I am already tired of my madness,

I take a step from your beak evening.
Our fist whitens, I am lying down,
you are bleeding, still standing,
you are drunk with my bitterness.
Your shadow is disappearing from you.

                              Solve me the exterior angle
at this vertex of a cyclic
quadrilateral we have created
when I march downstairs,
I do not listen or read your pronouncement, I feel plunge
like any old bull-dog, I walk slowly across a peculiar
message to defend your beautiful daughter-in-law,
you call Rainbow Williwaws to stop in my direction.
She is full, bold grey eyes, she is standing up for
the accused. "Can I see the full page for myself?"
She demands her completeness you are   sharing
with a woman, who interrupts her growth any time
she wants to breathe from my gazing into the future.

The Great Synagogue
is on fire, I am wishing
*   the sweetest bloom*
on the earth.
Black eyebrows over the arch.

There can be little doubt between us
when I manage my role in this life
as Sisyphus, who stops time to hurry up,
I work as an actor in a kabuki drama in the evenings
and spend the whole day fishing shad from Newfoundland
to Florida, I carve the warmth of affection, however,
I unlock the door because I know the housework
she has to add to the silence she spends in the office,
I need nothing to further the interference. Because I am
silent in a room. I unlock myself.

                    She recognizes, however,

that my body is still the smoke
from the burnt,

into a ghetto
I am forced to complete
our priesthood apprenticeship,

we clear
the debris
of a demolished post office,

we gather
and destroy
classical Russian books in the minds.

A local mayor
mitrages
the harsh winds and has been missed for good.

Sorry is the silver,
is the silence,
is the face,

glistening in sweat,
I say each time
I fall from a height.

It is the nugget
that needs
brotherly shaping

when I do not mean much
to be burnt
as sorry.

Sorry
is the cooked name,
is the iron that is never hot,
I say and say
each time I miss a step,
I begin life afresh.

Midwinter night
I am falling
from the floating staircase,

I am falling
in the blizzard,
blithely
ignoring myself,
hanging
from nothingness.

I say the word
Sorry
that does not mean
sorry
because the word sorry
is burnt as the Final Solution.

                    One of my tongues is Slovak.
One of my tongues is gypsum plaster,
one of my tongues is coniferous,
one of my tongues is a saw,
one of my tongues is smouldering,
evening, mist, with a very long tongue,
I am licking the wounds of Hatshepsut, my self-portraits in the funerary
temple of hills,
several complex tongues are reinforced behind doors and windows,
I am a chameleon,
I am a wick smouldering in a corner of uncompleted house,
I am a thin shadow searching for a form,
I have assumed power over myself,
I am a sole power in my weakness with

the shape of your woman
in the mind to be above
the sky painted in watercolour
is closer to an egg in the single hand

you have carved from a marble
in a dry valley of breeding ground
for green snakes, wild birds, rare insects
in a chain of hunting,

we have come on time to buy
for a European gallery.

How much do you make
after adding the bric-a-brac

when just thinking how discouraging
it could have been to fall
on the face of plummets?
I have imagined the possibilities.

You are busy and involved
in this mould instead of watching
your back to see how far you have gone,
you require no schedule.

Whether to sell this your provision
for the next day salvation
or not you do not want to know
because we try to avoid stress.

Being afraid of some impending disaster,
you have refused to eat and drink
without a specific date in mind
to weave and weave.

I am gladly to stand up
on my leglessness for you
when I answer to the baseless taunts,
we do not give out working the spirit.

Think of the thousands
who have seen you in the breakages
in France, Spain, elsewhere,
sometimes you are frustrated

or disappointed being viewed too much
you have no mouth to speak
and avoid distractions,
thanks that you are artifact

with a fascinating account
about a day in the missionary work
and not to be breathalysed
in the mixed smoke of the white buffoons.

If I were Caligula among the banana trees this wet morning

all the grass abandoned on the fence would be forced
to grow cheerfully and bloodily and complete their full length
they have been prevented from for a long time in the rain.

I would but I would be, yes, I would,

I have painted a space inside a watermelon,
it is that I do not know how to eat it well and take
good care of myself after I have added blue pigment
to the second room of your thought about how to cremate
the remains still lying nakedly on the floor with chains
in their necks from the lavatory open to the man
sitting on a rocking chair for all these years.

When your love is declined what do you do next?
For me I colour the sky with crayons out of the deepest
of your colour-blind, is something to search for as money
in the darkest depths of your dreams, you hold your breath
and my smiles thinking all is well now for the nonsense.
I have seen myself falling in love with the rain, it is raining,
it is almost midnight, I have clothed myself with the darkness
sitting inside a word of seed husk, I watch people
who are watering my thoughts, I think something is adding up
to my names
I am sturdy legs with sharp, powerful talons,
I am a whining sound as the air,
rushing through its widespread pinions,
I am black hawk soaring, soaring skyward
I respond to the unceasing molecular motions
of the air particles from your anger among the bad birds,
I am a

Your men are back home from a long war.
They look chagrined.
The chaffinch among them cannot chainsaw his spirit.

He cerises his position with chalybeate water.
His CH is clear, colourful and lightening,
their women know that, the figures inside are not the same
as those in the uniforms,
they wait for the cesspool to be exposed
elsewhere in the ceremonial grounds.

You have dressed them with sunflowers
show them in the streets to mark the zenith of your pride,

after Philip Guston's "Head-Double View".

This the progress. Progress here means
moving away from figurative works
towards abstraction. This is honest art or pure art.
But you are getting sick and tired of all that purity.
Because you want to tell stories. Because you want
freedom and "avoid the blithe commerciation of Pop
Art." You have said, "We are image-makers and image-
ridden." However, the gravity of these sinister heads,
hands, ordinary boots, clocks, sandwiches, is to finish
yourself with figures in Ku-Klux-Klan-like hoods.

What is art? Is it a journey to bring to life energy
and vitality of the mind and heart that making the simple
lines and colours of object in distilling form? or to mirror
unbalanced men, scoundrels, thieves, prostitutes, drunkards,
stupid dreamers, unhealthy peasants, degraded workers,
unclean bourgeois, cowardly soldiers, avaricious ministers,
feeble artists, hysterical priests showing full of drawings?
You and I are facing the same challenge and sometimes
I feel like stopping painting all together in my return
to abandon simple lines and capture the movement of today.
I sketch and draw to fill the space I have left behind

the earth.

This earth is taking its shape
in earthquakes, tsunamis,
fires, floods, volcanoes,
tornadoes, typhoons, hurricanes.

This whole difficult step
to your future nears its end.
Putting up with the wrath
of emotional distress,
let my pain be the August sun
in the autumn rains.
Let my faith roll silently
in the noisy streets.
Still, let me be a bolt of lightning
striking me with cancer.
Stepped in with an oath,
yellow blossom remains
two unchangeable things:
scarecrow harvesting
and singing of the male crickets.

Oh yeah! Do they come by a camel caravan
carrying guns, and say,
                              Hoeveel kosi het om deze
film te ontwikkelen? Ik ben de weg kwijk.
Waar zijn de toiletten? Where is the isolated lake?
And quickly take your pockets and walk away?

I hear black immigrants are taking every job away.
Do they hide in the street corners of Angel Angles
and when you walk home from work with a whore,
they seize your throat with knives and say:
Guv, I want your job?

On your TVs, I have seen everything myself.
How your grampus-street makers have graffitied
their faces and bodies of transplanted surgically pigments:
"Black Immigrants Have Stolen Our Jobs. Thiefs! Ga Weg! Help!"
An actor manque leads the gravy train.

An actor manque leads the gravy train,
this is goody- goody for the little heavens,
I goggle with eyes of your godson,
your golden boy displays his grapevine byo burning goods and lives,
they guzzle with laughter when I puzzle to cross a paved road.

Another morning. Very dry.
The sun is out there long time.

The calls have started.
You have nothing to offer.
They cannot take this.
You are growing too old every second.
Yes. You must!
The people around you
are impatient.
They take an hour a year.

They shout and insult,
reporting you to strangers
who have never washed their faces before.
Still you keep your smile of a mask on
and take your move
in the mesh of mud and sand.
I know you say to yourself:
Do not hurry me!
I do not think of figures or time,
think of people!

No blame! No head or chest!
It is just this empty figure
that sits at the curio table does not know
whether to write or sip hot oolong tea,
you are wearing this
and you are dying for,
the campaign to colour you
the callousness
and the worse, the composite
of restive restaurant.

We are rogues.
That is what your other self says.
You have accepted this role-play
and run the risk to have the money
in the bank though the time is over
and have a riveting movement
after sleepless hours.
Because it is respectful
to stand up and keep
your grooming in order.

I paint Sunday with your smiles
and you yearn for a day to see

new things of metaphors every where.
Yes. God is waiting for the right time.
Because one minute passes the fence
and the noun sentence is a word,
be patient not making
hasty decisions or overeating,
still waiting to answer your puzzles
in Eden. Wednesday. Icy rains falling,
do not confuse patience
with inattentiveness or apathy.
Because the sky is still white filled with snow,
tell your neighbours to meet us for lunch.

I slow to fulfill my promises.
Leave your prayers at my doorsteps.
Let me be occupied with works I am assigned.
Let my works lead me to waters of life.

Nature Francis

1.

Pretty Field

A big flower plant grows in the space.
Its leaves are black and white hair,
angry birds hang on it with a mass
of intensely shining yellow leaves
of great length coiled up on its
branches from the horizon,
I have clipped my moustache
to allow male birds who are
mixed up with the women in
the clouds to share escape
route, the absolutely monstrous
situation, again in your tenses.
When the remark is always
of insupportable stupidity,
I simply bow my head.

Under this long canopy of hair
all the clumsy stubbornness
is poised, precisely waiting
for the parts where the drips
hang, I call for your great delicacy,
my frozen foot-roots begin
and railway is built in a stone,
I spend your passion

                a privilege never used

before for Lysander's blood,
your mother says, she is not
guilty with your doublet tongues
that call all the girl prostitutes in
to measure the debt that
the bankrupt sleeper
has mistaken quite
these night mortals as

                nailbars emerging from

another cheap labour camp,

I keep the museum of gulags
in check in your pages.

For awhile I remain
your tender when I am
dead or alive, or numbness,
your carcass to my hounds,
my hounds to your birds.

I earn a dollar in some
slight measure it will pay.

Now when the sky is brutally
exploited, the birds are dragged
with their fluid fire of frightening
circumstances, the coal dust
remains exploded in your head,
in your memory, I go look for
confounding oath on oath,
I will not lie for being awake,
your girlfriend becomes
a coast of fresh blood.

Is this activity a work
or a hobby? Or both?
Joseph Brodsky paid
the price for building
these wheel and axle principles.
We too are ready to do the same
for this block and tackle.
That is why I sing
the Mandelstam hymns
and I work hard
to remember
my Russian accent.
I do not want to say
I am not speaking
of shedding any other guilty
act elsewhere in the turbine room.
Because the blades are clearly visible,
are uniformly distributed as
internal molecular energy
among these immigrates
from Africa and Middle East
at the same temperature
of what you earn.
Remember, black Africans
are killed in South Africa

for stealing work.
So what is work?
You ask me, you ask again.
Because we pray that this
mixture must burn and expand,
hence four-stroke cycle we build
with the minds of the slaves,

                    no downward pull

of the string on the support,
bosses study the diagrams
we have worked on for nearly
two decades with your energy,
diagrams of a cylinder and valves,
the valve operation gears,
action carburetors, we spend
the whole day fixing your heat,
I drop my sugar tongs down.
We neglect friction at the fulcrum.
I hear the clanking of their spoons
in the buckets for the builders,
who live in the tents between
fear and hope, you start to
erect yourself again at a post,
a well-bred voice on the night air
is coming back to you,
I remark with your relish
when we are taken back
from ourselves as a deep draught,
I grant all your tribe to get much support
from your own mountainous memory,
Because beyond money,
I accomplish my work,
I accomplish my life.

                  I accomplish my work;

that twist in the space,
I am a commuter
in a train full of commuters,
I am going to complete that
installation of angry birds
left behind by an absent artist,
I am sure at your present
to own a different imagination,
a bold perception that will be
justified while I set your face
again from faces in this train
I manage in my sketchbook,
I take your menace so bravely
and make sure that when every
passerby is happily enough
shaking off by your little plash
in an inconsequent question.
I do not say much to you
but to observe with some decision,
where we try being proof
against each other
and everything we touch
for another attestation,
that you mean to understand
in short at first,
I keep holding
the thread with a woman
from a previous relationship.

I will skin my distance off,
I will get you your coloured finger right
with no foundation, no support,
only Sundays for remarkable things,
only the dealer in used clothes,

who refuses to believe that
you have thousand miles in the air
I must cover from my end,
I iron these nightmares
and she runs downstairs
to open the door for those
coming in so that she can
feed her three children
from exhaustion and pains.

What I find on sale this morning
is the hands of the old pawnbroker,
I draw out some curtains between us,
I hurry up and come out.
There you are!
You are now at
the peak of your career
and you must remember
your guest, who is looking
for a work to do in this yellow city,
who yearns to be a cook, haulier,
or an observer with astrophysical
observatory, or a designer of models
for the National Physical Laboratory,
I keep testing a ship model
in the sea-keeping tank ahead of him
when he spends his night sleeping
on the living-room couch,
he looks at the sick pictures
on the wall, the children
in this house tell him that
these pictures are angels
with your fresh little jaw,
who have lost their way
up there in search of work.
Sometimes he wants to slap
them on the face, but remains
himself that, he is still a guest
looking for a work and does not
want to commit any immortal crime.

Noontide. He walks
other part of this world,
through a narrow street,
telling himself that, I am not
meant to wound anybody, when
a daughter of Sunday sits somewhere
above everything I have seen here,
who is staring at him,
who is eating her bread
and sipping a hot drink,
he looks shambles in
a glass door of an office
he is passing by, he will
not have rued his bloody
blunder more than the phrase
of miracles he saw this morning
with precision and cool emotions.
Though this haulage is hateful
and it remains the one with
hat trick you are enjoying,
the hoax of your hoar frost,
you go straight from your start
to your midlife and not
to infrequently quit
yourself in a manner
quite as abrupt
and unexpected,
you do not choose
to consider all this.
That is why I am not
involuntarily spilling
half myself from the tea cup
we are into the saucer,
I do not choose to consider,
whether we are to expect
your returns or not when

I ponder conjectures about
new situations without
complete structures
to present them,
I keep your void,
wandering across
my brain with a day's
business of tranquility.
I am to get more kitchen
hands from the contents
you share with your pupils,
I invite your guest and your son,
I hope I am not mistaken myself,
I help you to another bun to refill
your mug with milk and the maid
brings it to commence operations.
I begin to fill a strange chill
in my soul, further than
receiving my first salary,
I am grateful for such
respectful and kind
treatment after this
hard work in the drains,
I feel the immediate beauty
of those angry birds hanging
above your time when it is
no more their exigency when
they have exfoliated you,
I cross the fuddled light
I used to enrich a harridan,
I am not failing my heart
I am actually permitting
myself to experience,
we manage the fjord
to the field in panic dew
with a pleasant start
of affection you have
followed for many years.

2.

Inland Terrain

Somewhere in the loom,
somewhere in the plankton systems,
where people are compelled works,
where I am somewhere
reflecting the inland terrain,
I usually have triangular
or round, solid stems,
I thrive in the marshes
or swamps, or your bond.
Here I am a guest
to my suicidal thoughts.
Here I am obliged to meet
these relentless deadlines
so that I can meet you again,
you who have taken the lead.
You who suffer my absence,
you who feel like just
giving the trees in you out,
you loathe your life
at where I am emotionally drained
among the words glistening
with the sweat in the hair.
Build me to overcome
my desire to die

for I grapple with traps,
I reciprocate your love
by building up your hate,
I complete another work,
this human in jesting your view,
visions are crystallized,
those standing by are loathed
in your poison to strike their will.

I will shake my strength,
I always tell myself
when there is no more strength
than your weak prayers,
I take a few spoonful of boiled milk
and prepare my body
for the next work.
It is still morning,
I wear your hands like grooves,
I am to leave the house of my body,
I wrap up every brain in wet newspaper
and help you on with my pelisse,
I leave you behind,
you absent painter,
who is still in a shawl,
I pass through the public hall
and go out at the front door.
You are still looking at me,
I step on the gravel road
wetted in the morning sun,
the sodden is accordingly,
I enter the Cultivation Viewer building,
here you run a studio,
I can see the square
and the fountain for the first time
through this painting on the floor.
The materials are ready,
all looking at each other

and then at me, I fetch
these brushes for oil painting,
I prepare palette knives, maulsticks,
solvents and dippers, oil colours,
I pick 195 x 114 cm stretched canvas,
and after absorbing myself,
not yet a licensed uproar,
or that confusion of many voices,
I lift the blind and look out:
here this inland terrain.
Another satisfied hunger.

Here another satisfied hunger,
I have gotten a work nobody wants.

I spend the day in a corner
of your thought open to falsehood,
painting inland terrain;
I spend the night
selling coffee in the bar
that sits in the doorway
not far from some hours
from a sleep I cannot pay for.
Nobody appears to have anything
to say to me when I wear
my newest silk neckerchief
continually stained with paints.
I spend the day still
painting the inland terrain,
I indulge myself in flames,
I assemble crowd walking outside,

or, dashing through your uncomfortable body
not to belong to anybody again,
I wash the fire bursting out,
I spend the night selling coffee
when I think about the stammer,
how he presents himself
in this waltz I believe,
I am not looking back
from reposing any foolish confidence
where it is not deserved for a little while.
In the day I recompose my body.
In the night I destroy myself,
I mop the whole floor
to pay the next day rent.
I am left with water satchels
in your hands for good.
Because my sleeps value at €3000,
I show you the museum invoice.
Who pays for these?
And who leads this auction?

I am thinking of you tonight.
I am thinking of this work,
I am thinking of your works
in the hands of fat pigs
who are selling them
through Sotheby's
I think of my death
through this work.

So how many works
can I think of when I cross
the border between us?

I push your order away.
I push your beauty away.
I push your decisions out,
I walk across this payment for good.
You find this easier than before.
Because I am erasing the line
between work and hobby.
I add the props and costumes.
You do employer and I do employee,
we start doing a place without a work,
I watch you sinking
in a small town up the road.
This is my inland terrain.
This is my inland terrain.
This is my inland terrain.
This is my work.

3.

Naturally Horned by the Honey

(1). She has covered herself with the hurricane storms, almost a length
of tummy bar, and everywhere she steps, licks in rains, from waitress
to bathing babies and putting them to sleep, from engraver to painter,
from nurse to psychiatrist, from wife to mother, she is all there carefully
burning bright and right in order to keep herself awake, I screw the pitch.
She says she does not care if I am well-paid or not, because she has no
label for my inclination to apply from the foreground I pencil in solemn
depth, I am tormented by the contrast between your idea to alter any
sallow face from something ascetic in her look and my handiwork,
a little mathematics with frost in every work, even very plump damsel
as fair as waxwork, describable to the countenance, the look is always
puritanical. Perhaps a little softened, but still imparting pains and pleasures
to inflict or bestow either for good or bad, I will not defer attending
to her desire longer than everything is absolutely completed in this
equation, $xy = y$, is an algebra with a vector space and a certain
superciliousness, I seek to usher you into this library before I go upstairs.
Individuals and clients in the hall restrict role mobility for practitioners,
who are bored with their current work, are asking to return to different
roles from gatekeeping decisions to new arrangements, it is good,
you say, to keep hiding inside the husk of a seed, I respond after
a solution, the most recently sought, so that a modest space ultimately

funded in highly prespecified form, remains the ounce and relief .
I discover presently that your face is the face in my demented clumsiness
we paint together in my studio without talking about it. Your lips quiver. You
want to say something, something that is always to blunder down our steps,
I usurp my place and I continue to follow a thread of strain, perhaps
better than gold, I struggle to understand with your brains I have borrowed
and that has a nameless day, I wait for your New English wife
and black Mexican peasants in New Mexico to cross the border with
a great deal of money for another months with no supposition on
the subject of their ogre and ghoul when I run down into the library
to see the light they have hired from the foundry of beams of the lustrous
ripple. I look up, not observing you or her at first, who is hiding behind
my dazzled eyes, I remind myself that, I have forgiven you long time,
yet not in words, not outwardly unchanging, you try to upbraid, to make
a cut and paste from this floodgates in order to draw those who are reading
your history that they are to cross out all the plotting profligates, or rake
those who are simulating disinterested love and work, you tell me, I spare
you the trouble of much talking about these skeletons for sales, you
consider this again when I have no desire to expostulate, I fail to cut
a feeling for this passive look. You keep yourself back in a sort of shuddering
sigh and soon I receive my taste, I am revived, I am myself, I am quite
near to my body, I carry my whole body upstairs, I guess my reply rightly?

(2). Struggling flabbily with myself in burning away the memories you have
borrowed from your grandfather, I rise from the cold bed and run across
the floor, leaping from one record to another, I number the museum
invoice with black ink and you carefully join the investors to enjoy these
new products. The skeletons of my natives do not come to us at first.
Because they are labelled among the objects, which are at low level that
have never succeeded in getting to where more than a single faith
is built to lead the market price, I correct your wound when you are
swagger across a sudden skirmish sunlight from the backyard. Your thought
is slanting through strange differences which do exist but we are aware,
I wish we were not ask how we have arrived at this result when it is now
possible to sacrifice for this trade on our part of some portion of the
premium, where you have met with some large losses, I cannot have
the least objection to this collection because no business is ever done,
I sign the old yellow cartridge paper, I keep this beautiful morning as
a known partner to respond to a proposition they are preparing to
compose against every effort built. Your curator is indicted. We wait

for your return to cremate this collection and that will probably be quite
easy to extract a sort of beauty from our memories from the blackness
or ugliness of our souls, we set up harmless trade so long as that is
clean and orderly. But your interest of this passage is obviously falling
short, in that you want to pay yourself before the scene becomes open
or hopelessness, I say yes or no, I leave that peculiar message to you
to hang around when visitors coming in stand up for or not, I look up
into your face, which is changing from sacrifice to money, I like it better
in this way than other people's stuff you carry at home and at Sunday
schools that may have some variation in your health, I try this time to
replace all this in the bag of a miscellaneous collection of little objects
you have already emptied out. I am not sure I am doing this inducement
myself or with your help from within. I follow you with difficulty resurrected
thoughts. You have succeeded in laughing. In this sunlight in the evening
I walk along the main road over the railway and I watch the wet chairs
in your conversation for nearly half an hour. During all this time I am not
turning a new page to wonder how you breathe and are looking frightened
through the arch, your comparative silence is ensued. I lead your forlorn
hope of keeping this wor you receive yourself with calm that seems to
me more penetrating than my countenance and movements at the moment.

(3). We sit on a cement bench under a shaded tree, not far from the public
statues, I can see clearly the figure with his eyes which are red and puffy
from weeping, I tell her, how this statue used to be the first person to
produce a newspaper in this town by writing everything himself and copied
with black ink and everything was ready for the market. I tell her that, I was
one of the under-aged boys who carried the pieces in every corner of this life
and our parents chased us to throw the pieces away and hurried up to class.
There he stands with his short, pudgy fingers to welcome us back at home
after a long absence with his usual puerile jokes, as if he was still weeping.
I tell her energetically that I was employed in the morning as a stringer and
sacked in the evening. The editor asked me, Jacob, what is your religion?
I told him, I am non-conformist. How do you find this place? Very good and
stupid. She says, adding a red colour to her embroidery, how did you find
the sevenpenny entrance and, passing through quickly was a problem to
you? O, I do not know. Because I do not remember even handling a shilling.
I walked out the house of the bazaar. I found myself in a few people, who
were drew up beside an improvised bamboo platform I went into the front
parlour, observing voices that were not encouraging from his end where
he pointed out the necessity of dividing the clerk of the kitchen, the cooks,

and the porters that were under the Horse House and at either side of this
dark entrance after the intolerable delay of the train, I strode down Market
Street and there I answered few questions. I distributed my functions
that were uncertain and peculiar from the methods of affirmative love to
the commissions that were somewhat alarmed after coming in with his
servants, the housekeepers, the pages, and the housemaids, I was left
behind to my strange crouching figure. She inquires why. The answer is,
I was in the complicated passages to wander helpless by the time I was
pleased that others were viewing in this direction with his thoughtful eyes
from yet another official escapades. I sat down on the floors staring at
the clock, I looked inside his memory, his nightmare, his dream, when
the questions arose as to whether my argument was convinced to mount
the staircase from amiability to sternness. I glance swiftly at him again.
She has not moved her eyes still on me away. I look at him, she looks
at me. Under this blanket, she says, women are shrieking everywhere.
I leave my eyes behind, walk the lodge gates at six p.m. She speaks of her
best friend. I ask her, who that one is, she says, I am the one. I kiss her.
I unwrap up a bar of chocolate and put it in her mouth. I tell her to
remember that she is always my best friend, someone passing by shouts
at me, you porter, leave your wife behind and go work! A ship has docked.

Envoy to Paradise, Triptych

Left Panel: The Swing & the Fury

I jiggle,

        I leapfrog,

I hurdle.

In the concert hall I build my complete life
with gaslight, slip & metronome. I baritone,
the bamboo clouds are behind us. Audience   pushing ahead
down the darkness. It seems the uttermost   same
distance from birth, I follow a street, newly   printed.
I'm on the boundary between *who I'm today*
& who I was yesterday. The immigrants with
open memories & individuals have crossed a hundred miles
in your uncertainty. I see them standing where
I've left the sunshine carved in a statue, I clasp
my hands, wandering in that better mind of soil,
I plough, I imagine how delightful I'm to your feelings,
warm & enlivening in sky & a large difference

for another month usurps to make another glitter,
the soft, the ivy, a conflagration, putting too much
strength into this effort, that may rarely vary from
swinging to intense walking when everything becomes
exposed & palpitating, my place for being pushed
unceremoniously in a tumbler, or still gripping, or
to only one side, I proceed to accompany myself.
I hire my looks still under the trees & that dim
the lawn. I list up all my lives, scattered about
behind different barbed wire fences,
I take my turn & wait for definite orders
to leave my touch alone beyond endurance,
you can hardly bear the feeling that protects
you in my sheath, I'm grateful for your intimacy.
I don't know if we've arrived in town to wonder
my surroundings which are turning ghostly with
domestic desires. In another life, I offer you
your life with your own little house to yourself,
I manage its small rooms to provide imaginative
freedom & zest that are unnerving as intentions
among your excellent portraits of English forms.
That's why you succeed in scaling the steep extremely
when I stitch the pieces I'm together as midlife crisis
with a thread of spider web to give a new exemplary
exhibition at this department. I apprehend any leisure
for anything else I mark. I eliminate all blocks of bureaucracy
or of any bric-a-brac that plays the accompaniment in an affectionate
manner. I almost choke myself in these approaches to end our journeys
I've no attachments to stuff every figure I meet when I find a way
into your visage. I look up into many faces for gallantry, all are
too much jolted at the one place to the astonishment of the passersby
in the street. I hold some stations up here, still occupied, & dealing with
a thing from morning until I'm satisfactorily fed by the night, I keep my own
counsel I've known from my first work above forlorn state. I'm quite busy
with calculations of ways & means

        to take a full step from motives of expediency
to susceptible vanity.

I crash my thinking through the big headlines. I crash
my pungent aid between real mutual advantages.
I crash the distance between us.

I fret,

      I phish,

I pshaw.

I peddler the pedestal.
I peter

           with your wedding present.

I fix the brakes of this BMW
at the edge of the speed I gather.

I cross the three broken lines of dust.

(0).   The *first line* is a fishbone, covered by

two cottony puffs from white hair,
I play my execution with a good accent,

snarling above a cornet,
I slow down my tune among the motorcyclists.

I'm to pass the dairy farm
& discuss arthritis from your couch to a ladder.

I remember all the strays
you've included to manage the lowest rung of a leg,
enough hate is piled up on the boundary
that divides this small town.

A driver of that laundry truck dismisses the subject
& staggers heavily back up the aisle
with his eyes full of paraffin smoke,
he feels a hot tearing flames that points
his immediate outrage, flared up
in my swinging mood I become excited & distraught,
that I've disgraced myself,

                       leaving a chain of accidental circumstances

for a final link between our start & end,
& for that escapade,
that conservatism.

You may remember yourself if you ever grew up south of Robert States,
you've to wait for the damn 40 years to sign your name
before you can own your own house.
Because your name remains an item always tops
the list for men wearing gold-rimmed spectacles,
everything in the streets seems to sum you up for me,

             displaying the impossible manners.

(1).   The *second line* almost a baby equipment

& that requires assistances from the *sisters*.

I settle in the back seat,
waiting to see you in the mirror to measure

how the heart beat springs up & down
from your *South* to my *North,*

shaped on the anvil
with sugar sprinkles,

still under the summer heat
& irrational evasions are hanging from the sky,
a policy of deception.

In vain, I guess,
you keep yourself delightfully alive,
apparently with no calculated effort to encompass the baffling phenomena
of imaginative exercise,

                         the subject of unanswerable questions.

Open weeks are zipped
with your breath.

At this dead heat,
to pay the next death duty

for debris,
I debug the cancer

from the cactus wounds
with your fingers making numb.

The furthest corner of this room
is just a frown testimony from furrowing your brow,
once a Napoléon's skepticism.

I take the fury on your face
& fuse with the bones of the spine together with special Bantu settlements,

showing a brilliant future
in the *front* through the dark corridor.

(2).   The *third line* remains the surface underneath,

the glass is full to the brim.

I keep the brine
for a very agreeable weather

& that's why I'm not hurt
outside their dairy products
at the Cape, where Hottentots pay the "labour tax".

In Rome I make a long list,
age-old customs,

I cross an empty street I paint,
I walk through the ruins of Berlin Wall.

    This chess I play with you
in the shade that will be
in another brilliantly lit room,

I feel its akin to the street
I cross,
I've dreamt.
I cross the street of broken pieces
with painful memories painted in inconceivability,

I cross the street.
I spend those years in the slammer.
Remember the tartan room.
I share with you when you're in a quiet German voice,
when my soul is smouldering
& you spend your unblinking eyes
on my pure hatred,

you stare at that aghast
to dignify theory that covers your wants of apishness,
I've nothing against people making *money*

only that it lessens its appeal to a sense of wonder,

& paying *taxes* on it
for very tall for its age,
a place you're visiting.

This mound is the cladding among groups of people
in *heating allowance*.

I leave the clangour behind us
when we cross the boundary for good.

Middle Panel: Siting the Boundary of Conscience

1. AMIGO

Between two days
a gust
leaping clear.

2. ASHLAR

A ship crosses
its disc from azimuth,
I shape my babble
from other sides
within the kaleidoscope.

3. ASSAY

The captain builds a boundary of singleness for himself when he approaches
the doctor's cottage, where his profession is actually engaged in a poor
difference between his good friend & the doctor's daughters, he prepares his
mind from the repairs & embellishments to achieve a distinction of any
edifice that may be raised against him, he expresses himself in a reciprocal
style, he employs his fears he's owned from the distance for a few moments.
He comes away from many places of observation to avoid his shadow.

This part of his neighbourhood is wishing away in the sea current,

his income is doubled,

his pupilage is gratified,

the weight of the mind is an insupportable extent.

1. CORDITE

Standing with your legs
from the bay Aztecaly,
I take the late occurrences
of this serious remonstrance
as a vanishing amidst
far among the ridges,
a light springs up,
this boundary between us.
A mere alternation, you're
its daylight, I'm its shadow
fading away with you
along the marsh edges.
Now that you've allowed
me to rearranged the figures
in the mirror you've caught
in your gaslight in asymmetry
for the creation of a new work
for those who're climbing
the floating staircase,
I manage my effort with
a memory I've borrowed.
This structure remains the most

gift & a boundary algebra
but an ordinary thing.

        This is PA,
or the void
remains the explicit map
for group homology
for those in the streets,
who build A-valued functions
that are concatenated.
The result is always A Cross.

I've wrapped this prime
with your voice, full of love, that's
never added up to the sum
I mould into my hand,
I devour this ravenously
with your wet conscience
before I'm too distressing,
a recollection of the physical
suffering from total prostration.

2. CORNER SHOP

All day long the same grip of darkness.

***

My back has thickened with the twilight.

***

I draw myself to a perpetual evening.

3. COROLLA

That helix is glistening with the ruins of French Revolution.

This is the first lemma
we compose —
hebdomadal hedge.

Its proof
gives a minute account
of that day,
the ground is damp
beyond the stiffened boundary.

1. LEVER

        Some things are almost
the symbols of U, X, Q, S, V, S, R, etc, are

        between our vector spaces.
Your wife proves their existence

        with my corollary, *Right,*
against any Renaissance pigments

        on the walls or from the ceilings.
We remain silence behind the headlights.

2. LIFE SCIENCES

          Labour Day —
doing all this over again
at cross purposes.

3. LOGARITHM

          Aiming straight
from a logbook,
another light year.

1. SEMIBREVE

At the crag ahead of us,
a particular wish to see.

2. SENESCENCE

In the deepest slumber,
there remains
no immortality for man.

3. SENTINEL
Beyond the gulf of spiritual endeavours, it seems every fibre in my frame is
attaining full completion when a deadly locution is

          seizing your moment.

We gather hands which are folded together,
days are rushed away

        up the corridor
to complete the triangles

        for this trench.

  1. VELLUM

    It's quieter there
    though you clench your fists. It's still quieter here in a slowing speech,
    I replace yesterday with today or future, so that the waterwheel
    remains in no addition or subtraction for the horology. No boundaries
    when I forge a tongue from different tongues.
    Your gospel is nailed to a man's footsteps in the wet sand.
    I can hear the sea, which has been folded from its position,
    I can see its white babbling very far away.
    Now that we can touch the ship
    in the dry sand with our bare hands,
    I wait to hear breath
built around a circuitous route
to avoid the hill centre.

You DIY, this mesh,
without all this hassle at work,

DJ does his chance
by just standing there –
doing something!

  2. VENN DIAGRAM

I consider this old chrysalis
struggling to be christened,

I've found its half a member
of the workhouse, tormenting
with letters for money, I see
you under a wreath of hawthorn
bloom when chrome handles
become unmarked states,
the visitors begin
to filter into the hall,
a square of you from
the lower outline of visage
fills the features I've traced
on the paper that's not quite
in a question to build a boundary.

3. VERBAL NOUN

Holding water
from the goof ground,
I let the next finch
exist between my left
& right hands.

A finicky eater
flutters about,
chasing itself
beneath the other sheets
in a sketch.

the lake is wide
opened in your mouth

we gob the results,
hanging from hunches,

I decollate to the fuselage
without my go-cart.

A whirlwind of the boundary,
of every activity, is left behind.

Right Panel: Cooler towards Decaying

We're boundaries.
We're boundaries
built & broken.

                   We're built
as whales of bulwark
into categories. My boundary
is a whirlwind. We name it
cadenza, I calcify its reflection.

We're boundaries of monasteries,
libraries, main squares, monuments,
opera houses, old cities, beaches,
built & broken, we're boundaries.

We're boundaries, a calculated calamine,
in the stocks of the morning
to be threatened to grow,
momently darker,
attaching undue
importance to
whatever rigorous exercise
I apply through giggling,

we're boundaries, these lizards,
more dissatisfied, more sourly
expressive of disappointment;
we're lizards to our ends,
hiding behind white walls
we've built with all our strength;
we're lizards during the fall
above the bog in our wounds.
We break through every boundary
& turn H upside down.
That's why in our world,
there's no gap between
the servant & his master,
the lender & the borrower,
the creditor & the debtor,
I'm completely emptied
when everything is completely plundered,
the passage withers in tambourines.
Where wattles are covered with clay,
where the noise of the revelers in the street
remains our hiding place in your presence,
we're formed from no supposition
on any subject governing the guard,
we're staggers through the burst,
I go ahead about your story,
that doesn't agree with
what the historians have said
before your large audience,
I keep out, yes, out your way.
No eating an ogre or a ghoul,
no begging your pardon, sir,
I keep the edges to a pinch,
as I've been accustomed to do,
I feel disposed to see inside
& enter the house & retreat
from the floating staircase,
I master its ritzy riser, if that's
possible to alight the cuttings
for the next collage on dust.
Because this music is much more akin
to blue jazz than cold rock,

here within, you're easy reach.
I'm escaping with your attendee,
who escorts the doormen through the loopholes,
I'm escaping for good,
I find that everything that's
outrageously strange
fascinates me even when
I abominate that, or it leaves
a certain macabre appeal.
How do you react to the news
when they shout & boo?
A colleen grabs your wrist
& some paddies have a very
bad reaction to these peanuts.
I sit down to read your hand-
writing full of role-play,
a robin stares at a fishing rod
still in the lagoon to rob you
your self-confidence over the fire,
I justify nothing, only the touch,
the softness & the impossible.
Think of the dark sea washing away
all the remains of every border
we've broken behind us, think of the mathematics
we solve in this phrases, think of the wall
we're building between day & night
& that'll be soon turned into powder,
think of the border between
mathematics & poetry we've broken,
think of the border between experience
& imagination we've torn into apart,
think & think incredulously, think.
That's why I master no border between humans,
between nationalities, between colours, between opinions,
between classes, I empty the giant dustbins of my heart,
where your horizon is ringed completely
by ugliness, so frightful
& so arresting industrialism,
I get a little further away
from this slow moving flames of sulphur,

I retain its hummocky surface.
I remain a boundary, built & broken.

www.ingramcontent.com/pod-product-compliance
Lightning Source LLC
Chambersburg PA
CBHW081156130726
47996CB00009B/3151